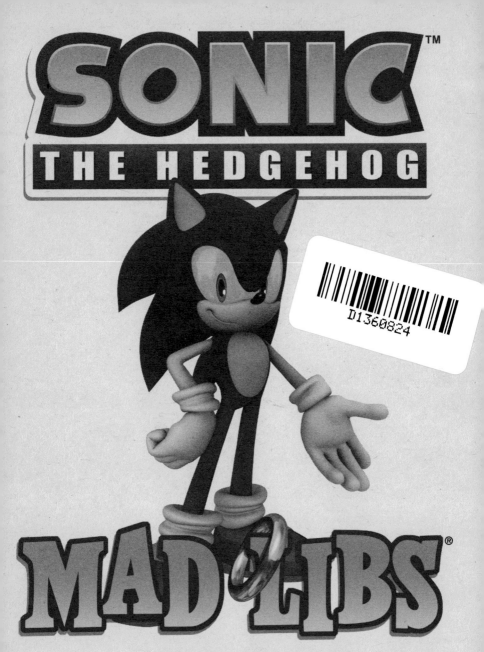

SONIC™
THE HEDGEHOG

MAD LIBS®

by Rob Valois

Mad Libs
An Imprint of Penguin Random House

MAD LIBS
Penguin Young Readers Group
An Imprint of Penguin Random House LLC

Concept created by Roger Price & Leonard Stern

Published by Mad Libs,
an imprint of Penguin Random House LLC,
345 Hudson Street, New York, New York 10014.
Printed in the USA.

ISBN 9780515158076
1 3 5 7 9 10 8 6 4 2

MAD LIBS

INSTRUCTIONS

MAD LIBS® is a game for people who don't like games! It can be played by one, two, three, four, or forty.

• RIDICULOUSLY SIMPLE DIRECTIONS

In this tablet you will find stories containing blank spaces where words are left out. One player, the READER, selects one of these stories. The READER does not tell anyone what the story is about. Instead, he/she asks the other players, the WRITERS, to give him/her words. These words are used to fill in the blank spaces in the story.

• TO PLAY

The READER asks each WRITER in turn to call out a word—an adjective or a noun or whatever the space calls for—and uses them to fill in the blank spaces in the story. The result is a MAD LIBS® game.

When the READER then reads the completed MAD LIBS® game to the other players, they will discover that they have written a story that is fantastic, screamingly funny, shocking, silly, crazy, or just plain dumb—depending upon which words each WRITER called out.

• EXAMPLE (*Before* and *After*)

"_____!" he said _____
    EXCLAMATION   ADVERB

as he jumped into his convertible _____ and
                                          NOUN

drove off with his _____ wife.
                      ADJECTIVE

"**OUCH**!" he said **STUPIDLY**
    EXCLAMATION   ADVERB

as he jumped into his convertible **CAT** and
                                            NOUN

drove off with his **BRAVE** wife.
                      ADJECTIVE

In case you have forgotten what adjectives, adverbs, nouns, and verbs are, here is a quick review:

An **ADJECTIVE** describes something or somebody. *Lumpy, soft, ugly, messy,* and *short* are adjectives.

An **ADVERB** tells how something is done. It modifies a verb and usually ends in "ly." *Modestly, stupidly, greedily,* and *carefully* are adverbs.

A **NOUN** is the name of a person, place, or thing. *Sidewalk, umbrella, bridle, bathtub,* and *nose* are nouns.

A **VERB** is an action word. *Run, pitch, jump,* and *swim* are verbs. Put the verbs in past tense if the directions say PAST TENSE. *Ran, pitched, jumped,* and *swam* are verbs in the past tense.

When we ask for **A PLACE**, we mean any sort of place: a country or city (*Spain, Cleveland*) or a room (*bathroom, kitchen*).

An **EXCLAMATION** or **SILLY WORD** is any sort of funny sound, gasp, grunt, or outcry, like *Wow!, Ouch!, Whomp!, Ick!,* and *Gadzooks!*

When we ask for specific words, like a **NUMBER**, a **COLOR**, an **ANIMAL**, or a **PART OF THE BODY**, we mean a word that is one of those things, like *seven, blue, horse,* or *head*.

When we ask for a **PLURAL**, it means more than one. For example, *cat* pluralized is *cats*.

MAD LIBS® is fun to play with friends, but you can also play it by yourself! To begin with, DO NOT look at the story on the page below. Fill in the blanks on this page with the words called for. Then, using the words you have selected, fill in the blank spaces in the story.

Now you've created your own hilarious MAD LIBS® game!

GOTTA GO FAST

ANIMAL _____

NOUN _____

COLOR _____

NOUN _____

NUMBER _____

CELEBRITY _____

PLURAL NOUN _____

VERB _____

PLURAL NOUN _____

ADJECTIVE _____

PERSON IN ROOM _____

NOUN _____

ADJECTIVE _____

TYPE OF FOOD _____

ADJECTIVE _____

NOUN _____

PART OF THE BODY _____

ADJECTIVE _____

MAD LIBS®

GOTTA GO FAST

Sonic the Hedge-_____ is a Sonic _____ with
        ANIMAL   NOUN

_____ fur. He is the fastest _____ around and can
   COLOR   NOUN

run _____ miles an hour. _____ the Hedgehog also
      NUMBER   CELEBRITY

has super-powered _____ and can _____ better
                        PLURAL NOUN   VERB

than almost anyone else. Sonic is able to harness the power of the

Chaos _____, which are _____-powered crystals that
         PLURAL NOUN   ADJECTIVE

allow him to transform into Super _____. Sonic may be a/an
                                    PERSON IN ROOM

_____, but he doesn't just use his _____ abilities for fun,
   NOUN   ADJECTIVE

he uses them to defeat his enemies, such as Dr. _____-man.
                                                  TYPE OF FOOD

And he does it all with a/an _____ smile and a confident
                               ADJECTIVE

_____—even though some people think that his _____
   NOUN   PART OF THE BODY

is too big. One thing is for certain: Sonic is definitely a/an _____
                                                               ADJECTIVE

hero.

MAD LIBS® is fun to play with friends, but you can also play it by yourself! To begin with, DO NOT look at the story on the page below. Fill in the blanks on this page with the words called for. Then, using the words you have selected, fill in the blank spaces in the story.

Now you've created your own hilarious MAD LIBS® game!

MILES PROWER'S TIME TO FLY

ADJECTIVE _____

NOUN _____

NOUN _____

CELEBRITY _____

NUMBER _____

NOUN _____

ADJECTIVE _____

NOUN _____

VERB ENDING IN "ING" _____

NOUN _____

ADJECTIVE _____

SILLY WORD _____

PLURAL NOUN _____

ADJECTIVE _____

NOUN _____

ADJECTIVE _____

COLOR _____

NOUN _____

MAD LIBS®
MILES PROWER'S
TIME TO FLY

Miles "Tails" Prower is one of Sonic's most _____ friends. He
                                                    ADJECTIVE

can build a/an _____ out of almost anything. Here are just a
                    NOUN

few of his inventions:

- After their flying _____ was destroyed by _____,
                          NOUN   CELEBRITY

   Tails built a better version named Tornado _____. This
                                                    NUMBER

   plane could transform its wings into a/an _____ shape
                                                    NOUN

   that allowed it to become extra _____.
                                        ADJECTIVE

- Not only is the Tornado an amazing _____, it can
                                            NOUN

   transform into a/an _____ robot with a/an
                          VERB ENDING IN "ING"

   _____ launcher! In this _____ form, the Tornado
        NOUN   ADJECTIVE

   is called the _____ and is one of Sonic's favorite
                      SILLY WORD

   _____.
        PLURAL NOUN

- Every fox needs a/an _____ ride. And Tails has created a
                            ADJECTIVE

   super-speedy _____ called the Whirlwind S7. This
                      NOUN

   _____ roadster is bright _____ and can jump over
        ADJECTIVE   COLOR

   almost every _____.
                      NOUN

MAD LIBS® is fun to play with friends, but you can also play it by yourself! To begin with, DO NOT look at the story on the page below. Fill in the blanks on this page with the words called for. Then, using the words you have selected, fill in the blank spaces in the story.

Now you've created your own hilarious MAD LIBS® game!

THE WORLD IS MINE

NOUN _____

NOUN _____

ADJECTIVE _____

NOUN _____

NOUN _____

ADJECTIVE _____

PLURAL NOUN _____

ADJECTIVE _____

NOUN _____

A PLACE _____

NOUN _____

PERSON IN ROOM _____

ADJECTIVE _____

PLURAL NOUN _____

ADJECTIVE _____

PLURAL NOUN _____

PERSON IN ROOM _____

ADJECTIVE _____

"I hate that _____!" Dr. Eggman screamed as Sonic raced by.

NOUN

"I will catch that _____-hog, if it's the last thing I do! And

NOUN

once that _____ Sonic's gone, the whole _____ will

ADJECTIVE NOUN

be mine to conquer!" The super-evil _____ has been known

NOUN

to ruin things that Sonic loves, especially nature and _____,

ADJECTIVE

fluffy _____. The _____ Dr. Eggman is a sinister

PLURAL NOUN ADJECTIVE

_____ who wants nothing more than to control (the)

NOUN

_____, even if it means destroying every single _____

A PLACE NOUN

on the planet in the process. And _____ has sworn to stop

PERSON IN ROOM

him and make the world _____ again. One of Dr. Eggman's

ADJECTIVE

favorite things to do is capture furry _____ and turn them

PLURAL NOUN

into _____ robots to help him collect Chaos _____.

ADJECTIVE PLURAL NOUN

But his greed is usually his undoing, as _____ uses this quality

PERSON IN ROOM

to defeat Dr. Eggman and his army of _____ robots.

ADJECTIVE

MAD LIBS® is fun to play with friends, but you can also play it by yourself! To begin with, DO NOT look at the story on the page below. Fill in the blanks on this page with the words called for. Then, using the words you have selected, fill in the blank spaces in the story.

Now you've created your own hilarious MAD LIBS® game!

NO TIME FOR GAMES

PART OF THE BODY (PLURAL) _____

PLURAL NOUN _____

ADJECTIVE _____

VERB _____

PLURAL NOUN _____

ADVERB _____

NOUN _____

NOUN _____

ADJECTIVE _____

NOUN _____

VERB ENDING IN "ING" _____

NOUN _____

PLURAL NOUN _____

ADJECTIVE _____

PLURAL NOUN _____

COLOR _____

ADJECTIVE _____

NOUN _____

MAD LIBS

NO TIME FOR GAMES

_____ the Echidna is one of Sonic's greatest
PART OF THE BODY (PLURAL)

_____. While Sonic is _____ and can _____
PLURAL NOUN   ADJECTIVE   VERB

at amazing speeds, Knuckles has spiky _____ that allow
                                        PLURAL NOUN

him to _____ climb over any _____. He is from
        ADVERB   NOUN

Angel _____ and is sworn to protect the Island's most
       NOUN

_____ item: the Master _____, which gives the
ADJECTIVE   NOUN

Island its _____ power. Without it, the floating
            VERB ENDING IN "ING"

_____ would crash into the tropical _____ below.
NOUN   PLURAL NOUN

Knuckles loves the Island and its many _____ environments,
                                         ADJECTIVE

such as sandy _____, deep _____ seas, and _____
               PLURAL NOUN   COLOR   ADJECTIVE

forests. For Knuckles, there's truly no _____ like home!
                                          NOUN

MAD LIBS® is fun to play with friends, but you can also play it by yourself! To begin with, DO NOT look at the story on the page below. Fill in the blanks on this page with the words called for. Then, using the words you have selected, fill in the blank spaces in the story.

Now you've created your own hilarious MAD LIBS® game!

SHADOW THE HEDGEHOG

ANIMAL _____

COLOR _____

ADJECTIVE _____

NOUN _____

ADJECTIVE _____

PLURAL NOUN _____

ADJECTIVE _____

NOUN _____

NOUN _____

ADJECTIVE _____

PLURAL NOUN _____

PERSON IN ROOM _____

VERB _____

PLURAL NOUN _____

PLURAL NOUN _____

MAD LIBS®

SHADOW THE HEDGEHOG

Imagine a/an _____ that's a mirror image of Sonic, only this
            ANIMAL

_____ -and-red hedgehog was created by a/an _____
  COLOR   ADJECTIVE

scientist and eventually released into the world by Dr. Egg- _____ .
                                                             NOUN

He's just like Sonic in many ways, except that Sonic is _____
                                                        ADJECTIVE

and likes helping _____, and Shadow the Hedgehog is
                  PLURAL NOUN

_____ and will use any _____ to achieve his goals. In
 ADJECTIVE   NOUN

fact, Sonic and Shadow are like day and _____. While Sonic is
                                        NOUN

super _____, Shadow has special _____ that
      ADJECTIVE   PLURAL NOUN

make him just as fast. Plus, Shadow would never open up his heart to

_____. As much as Sonic tried to teach Shadow to
PERSON IN ROOM

_____ others and that it was better to be one of the good
 VERB

_____, they would never be _____.
PLURAL NOUN   PLURAL NOUN

MAD LIBS® is fun to play with friends, but you can also play it by yourself! To begin with, DO NOT look at the story on the page below. Fill in the blanks on this page with the words called for. Then, using the words you have selected, fill in the blank spaces in the story.

Now you've created your own hilarious MAD LIBS® game!

STEP IT UP, PART 1

PERSON IN ROOM _____

ADVERB _____

ADJECTIVE _____

PLURAL NOUN _____

ADJECTIVE _____

PLURAL NOUN _____

A PLACE _____

ADJECTIVE _____

COLOR _____

NOUN _____

PLURAL NOUN _____

CELEBRITY _____

ANIMAL _____

ADJECTIVE _____

NOUN _____

VERB _____

A PLACE _____

PLURAL NOUN _____

MAD LIBS®

STEP IT UP, PART 1

"Out of my way, _____," Sonic called out as he _____
            PERSON IN ROOM   ADVERB

sped past one of his greatest rivals. Sonic was on his way to fight an

army of _____ robotic _____. The _____
         ADJECTIVE   PLURAL NOUN   ADJECTIVE

Dr. Eggman had been capturing the _____ of (the)
                                        PLURAL NOUN

_____ Island and turning them into _____ minions
   A PLACE   ADJECTIVE

to do his bidding. High above, Sonic could see Tails' _____
                                                            COLOR

plane, the _____, heading straight toward a cloud of evil
               NOUN

flying _____. Sonic didn't have time to worry about his
        PLURAL NOUN

friend because Metal _____ was blocking his path. This evil
                         CELEBRITY

_____ was almost as _____ as Sonic. As Sonic got
   ANIMAL   ADJECTIVE

close, he focused his energy and let loose a mighty _____
                                                         NOUN

Attack, knocking his adversary to the ground. Sonic wanted to stay and

_____, but he knew he had to get to (the) _____
   VERB   A PLACE

before all the _____ were destroyed.
                  PLURAL NOUN

MAD LIBS® is fun to play with friends, but you can also play it by yourself! To begin with, DO NOT look at the story on the page below. Fill in the blanks on this page with the words called for. Then, using the words you have selected, fill in the blank spaces in the story.

Now you've created your own hilarious MAD LIBS® game!

HAVE NO FEAR,
AMY ROSE IS HERE!

NOUN _____

PERSON IN ROOM _____

COLOR _____

VERB _____

NOUN _____

A PLACE _____

PLURAL NOUN _____

SILLY WORD _____

NOUN _____

ADJECTIVE _____

NOUN _____

EXCLAMATION _____

NOUN _____

VERB _____

NOUN _____

PLURAL NOUN _____

ADJECTIVE _____

PLURAL NOUN _____

MAD LIBS®
HAVE NO FEAR,
AMY ROSE IS HERE!

Amy Rose is a fun-loving _____ who has had a crush
                                    NOUN

on _____ for a long time. This _____ hedgehog
      PERSON IN ROOM   COLOR

would only _____ her crush from afar. But after many
                 VERB

adventures, she joined Team _____ and has sworn to protect
                                    NOUN

(the) _____ from evil _____ such as Dr. Eggman
         A PLACE   PLURAL NOUN

and his messenger, _____. In countless battles, Amy has
                        SILLY WORD

proven to be an amazing _____ and a/an _____
                              NOUN   ADJECTIVE

hero. Now she is a trusted _____ to Sonic. With a battle
                                 NOUN

cry of "_____!" Amy wields her signature weapon, the
            EXCLAMATION

imposing _____ Hammer, which has the power to _____
              NOUN   VERB

any _____ it strikes. When Amy's not fighting to defend weak
        NOUN

_____ from _____ bullies, she enjoys cooking up
   PLURAL NOUN   ADJECTIVE

delicious _____ for all her friends to enjoy.
               PLURAL NOUN

MAD LIBS® is fun to play with friends, but you can also play it by yourself! To begin with, DO NOT look at the story on the page below. Fill in the blanks on this page with the words called for. Then, using the words you have selected, fill in the blank spaces in the story.

Now you've created your own hilarious MAD LIBS® game!

BEHOLD THE POWER OF CHAOS EMERALDS

A PLACE _____

NUMBER _____

PLURAL NOUN _____

ADJECTIVE _____

PLURAL NOUN _____

ADVERB _____

NOUN _____

ADJECTIVE _____

PERSON IN ROOM (MALE) _____

ADJECTIVE _____

NOUN _____

COLOR _____

NOUN _____

PLURAL NOUN _____

ADJECTIVE _____

NUMBER _____

VERB ENDING IN "ING" _____

PLURAL NOUN _____

MAD LIBS®
BEHOLD THE POWER OF
CHAOS EMERALDS

In all of (the) _____, there are only _____ Chaos
        A PLACE   NUMBER

Emeralds. These mystical _____ are the most powerful and
               PLURAL NOUN

_____ items in the known universe. That is why heroes and
ADJECTIVE

their _____ will _____ battle to the ends of the
   PLURAL NOUN   ADVERB

_____ to possess them. Each emerald has _____
NOUN   ADJECTIVE

powers, but when _____ uses all seven together, he has
       PERSON IN ROOM (MALE)

the ability to transform into his super form called _____
                             ADJECTIVE

Sonic. In this form, his usually blue _____ becomes a brilliant
                    NOUN

_____ that makes him look like a glowing _____. In
COLOR   NOUN

the upgraded form, his already amazing _____ become
                       PLURAL NOUN

more _____ and he can jump _____ times higher.
ADJECTIVE   NUMBER

Sonic's _____ ability is also multiplied, making him
     VERB ENDING IN "ING"

able to deflect all kinds of deadly _____!
                    PLURAL NOUN

MAD LIBS® is fun to play with friends, but you can also play it by yourself! To begin with, DO NOT look at the story on the page below. Fill in the blanks on this page with the words called for. Then, using the words you have selected, fill in the blank spaces in the story.

Now you've created your own hilarious MAD LIBS® game!

TOGETHER, WE CAN DO ANYTHING!

ADJECTIVE _____

COLOR _____

CELEBRITY _____

NOUN _____

NOUN _____

NUMBER _____

ADJECTIVE _____

PERSON IN ROOM _____

TYPE OF FOOD _____

ADJECTIVE _____

PLURAL NOUN _____

ADJECTIVE _____

NOUN _____

ADVERB _____

NOUN _____

PERSON IN ROOM _____

ADJECTIVE _____

ADJECTIVE _____

MAD LIBS®
TOGETHER, WE CAN DO ANYTHING!

_____ and sweet, Cream is a/an _____ rabbit who
   ADJECTIVE   COLOR

tags along with Team _____ on their many adventures. Her
                               CELEBRITY

best friend is a/an _____ named Cheese who wears a/an
                           NOUN

_____-tie and is always willing to help out. Together, they've
   NOUN

been on _____ amazing escapades, but none more _____
         NUMBER   ADJECTIVE

than the one where they first met _____. Dr. Eggman had
                                 PERSON IN ROOM

kidnapped Cream and _____ from their _____
                    TYPE OF FOOD   ADJECTIVE

home. His plan was to capture all the Island's _____ and
                                        PLURAL NOUN

turn them into _____ robots to help build his _____
              ADJECTIVE   NOUN

Empire. Cream didn't know who would rescue them, until Sonic

_____ appeared and was able to free Cream and Cheese by
   ADVERB

defeating Dr. Eggman's Egg- _____-Tank. Once free, they
                                NOUN

helped Sonic rescue Cream's mother and _____ and drive
                                   PERSON IN ROOM

the _____ Dr. Eggman from the Island. After that, Cream
    ADJECTIVE

and Cheese were so _____, they joined up with Team Sonic.
               ADJECTIVE

MAD LIBS® is fun to play with friends, but you can also play it by yourself! To begin with, DO NOT look at the story on the page below. Fill in the blanks on this page with the words called for. Then, using the words you have selected, fill in the blank spaces in the story.

Now you've created your own hilarious MAD LIBS® game!

CHAO CHAO

ADJECTIVE _____

NOUN _____

PLURAL NOUN _____

ADJECTIVE _____

PLURAL NOUN _____

ADVERB _____

ADJECTIVE _____

PLURAL NOUN _____

ADJECTIVE _____

VERB _____

ADVERB _____

NUMBER _____

ADJECTIVE _____

VERB _____

NOUN _____

ADJECTIVE _____

ADJECTIVE _____

PLURAL NOUN _____

MAD LIBS

CHAO CHAO

What could be more satisfying than raising your own _____

ADJECTIVE

little _____? Many find that these adorable little _____

NOUN   PLURAL NOUN

make the best pets. The Chao come in many different forms and can

be found hidden away in their many _____ gardens with clean

ADJECTIVE

and pure _____, where they live _____ in innocent

PLURAL NOUN   ADVERB

bliss. These _____ creatures hatch out of _____

ADJECTIVE   PLURAL NOUN

and become _____ with the right amount of positive

ADJECTIVE

attention—although forgetting to _____ them or treating

VERB

them badly can _____ cause them to go dark. Chao can be

ADVERB

one of _____ alignments: Hero, Neutral, or even _____.

NUMBER   ADJECTIVE

To make a Chao _____, it must first enter into a/an _____

VERB   NOUN

and will then emerge more _____ than before. Chao Gardens

ADJECTIVE

can be found all over the world, such as Station Square or _____

ADJECTIVE

Gardens. Chao can also absorb the abilities of the _____

PLURAL NOUN

that they touch.

MAD LIBS® is fun to play with friends, but you can also play it by yourself! To begin with, DO NOT look at the story on the page below. Fill in the blanks on this page with the words called for. Then, using the words you have selected, fill in the blank spaces in the story.

Now you've created your own hilarious MAD LIBS® game!

FROGGY?

ADJECTIVE _____

VERB ENDING IN "ING" _____

A PLACE _____

PERSON IN ROOM _____

VERB _____

PLURAL NOUN _____

NOUN _____

VERB _____

A PLACE _____

ADVERB _____

NUMBER _____

NOUN _____

EXCLAMATION _____

ADVERB _____

ADJECTIVE _____

NOUN _____

EXCLAMATION _____

MAD LIBS®

FROGGY?

It was just another lazy day for _____ the Cat. As usual, he
ADJECTIVE

planned to spend his day _____ around (the) _____.
VERB ENDING IN "ING" A PLACE

But he couldn't find his friend _____ anywhere. Where
PERSON IN ROOM

could Froggy have gone? "You've gotta _____ me," Big said to
VERB

Sonic. "We have to find Froggy." "We'll get all the _____
PLURAL NOUN

to help look," replied Sonic. "Thanks," said Big. "I'll search the

_____, because sometimes Froggy likes to _____
NOUN VERB

there." "And we'll go search (the) _____," added Amy Rose.
A PLACE

After _____ searching for _____ minutes, Big saw a
ADVERB NUMBER

giant robotic _____ marching away in the distance.
NOUN

"_____!" Sonic shouted. "It's Dr. Eggman. He must have
EXCLAMATION

Froggy!" Big _____ ran off after the _____ robot. "Big,
ADVERB ADJECTIVE

wait!" cried Amy as she raced back. On her shoulder was a familiar

green _____. "_____!" croaked Froggy as he
NOUN EXCLAMATION

watched his friend run off.

MAD LIBS® is fun to play with friends, but you can also play it by yourself! To begin with, DO NOT look at the story on the page below. Fill in the blanks on this page with the words called for. Then, using the words you have selected, fill in the blank spaces in the story.

Now you've created your own hilarious MAD LIBS® game!

STEP IT UP, PART 2

ADJECTIVE _____

NOUN _____

PERSON IN ROOM _____

ADJECTIVE _____

COLOR _____

PLURAL NOUN _____

ADJECTIVE _____

NOUN _____

ADJECTIVE _____

ADVERB _____

PLURAL NOUN _____

ADJECTIVE _____

NUMBER _____

ADVERB _____

PLURAL NOUN _____

ADJECTIVE _____

PERSON IN ROOM _____

MAD LIBS

STEP IT UP, PART 2

Tails looked out over the side of his _____ flying _____.
                                        ADJECTIVE   NOUN

On the ground below, he saw his friend, _____, fighting the
                                           PERSON IN ROOM

_____ Metal Sonic. He wanted to help his _____
   ADJECTIVE   COLOR

friend, but he had problems of his own. A flock of flying robotic

_____ were heading his way, and they looked _____.
   PLURAL NOUN   ADJECTIVE

He flipped a switch, and a mighty _____ launched from the
                                       NOUN

bottom of the plane. It sailed into the center of the _____
                                                         ADJECTIVE

flying robots, who _____ swarmed around it. The explosion
                      ADVERB

was meant to destroy the _____, but the robots just
                            PLURAL NOUN

absorbed the _____ energy and grew to _____ times
                ADJECTIVE   NUMBER

their original size. Tails _____ dived his plane to avoid crashing
                              ADVERB

into the giant flying _____. Luckily, now that the robots
                         PLURAL NOUN

were huge and _____, they were also slow. But he would need
                 ADJECTIVE

_____'s help to defeat Dr. Eggman.
 PERSON IN ROOM

MAD LIBS® is fun to play with friends, but you can also play it by yourself! To begin with, DO NOT look at the story on the page below. Fill in the blanks on this page with the words called for. Then, using the words you have selected, fill in the blank spaces in the story.

Now you've created your own hilarious MAD LIBS® game!

LEGENDARY WIND MASTER

ADJECTIVE _____

VERB ENDING IN "ING" _____

ADVERB _____

VERB (PAST TENSE) _____

ADJECTIVE _____

NOUN _____

ADVERB _____

NOUN _____

A PLACE _____

ANIMAL (PLURAL) _____

NUMBER _____

NOUN _____

PART OF THE BODY _____

NUMBER _____

VERB _____

ADJECTIVE _____

NOUN _____

MAD LIBS®

LEGENDARY WIND MASTER

"You think you're _____? Well, you look slower than a/an

_____ turtle from up here," Jet the Hawk _____

VERB ENDING IN "ING"   ADVERB

cried out as he _____ over Sonic. "Oh yeah?" replied

                VERB (PAST TENSE)

Sonic. "You think you're as _____ as me? Well, why don't we

                    ADJECTIVE

race to that _____ over there." Jet smirked _____ as

         NOUN   ADVERB

he circled back. "And when I'm the winner, you'll have to admit that

I'm the fastest _____ in (the) _____," he shouted.

             NOUN   A PLACE

"Don't count your _____ before they're hatched," Sonic

                   ANIMAL (PLURAL)

shouted back. Then he added, "I've beaten you _____ times

                                 NUMBER

before, and I plan to wipe that _____ off your _____

                   NOUN   PART OF THE BODY

one more time." "Okay, on the count of _____," Jet said as he

                            NUMBER

lined up next to Sonic. "Three, two, one! _____!" The two

                               VERB

_____ speedsters took off. Only one _____ could be

    ADJECTIVE   NOUN

the winner!

MAD LIBS® is fun to play with friends, but you can also play it by yourself! To begin with, DO NOT look at the story on the page below. Fill in the blanks on this page with the words called for. Then, using the words you have selected, fill in the blank spaces in the story.

Now you've created your own hilarious MAD LIBS® game!

NEVER GET ON BLAZE'S BAD SIDE

NOUN _____

NOUN _____

A PLACE _____

NOUN _____

ADJECTIVE _____

PART OF THE BODY _____

SILLY WORD _____

ADJECTIVE _____

NOUN _____

NUMBER _____

PART OF THE BODY _____

NOUN _____

PLURAL NOUN _____

ADVERB _____

PLURAL NOUN _____

ADJECTIVE _____

ADVERB _____

NOUN _____

MAD LIBS®
NEVER GET ON
BLAZE'S BAD SIDE

"The _____ Emerald will be mine!" Dr. Eggman cried
       NOUN

out as his robotic Egg-_____ stomped its way through
           NOUN

(the) _____, destroying every _____ in its path.
   A PLACE   NOUN

"Not if I stop you!" called out the _____ purple cat, Blaze.
         ADJECTIVE

Blaze pointed her fiery _____ at Dr. Eggman, who laughed a
    PART OF THE BODY

loud "_____." Then his _____ robot transformed
   SILLY WORD   ADJECTIVE

into a giant _____ with _____ spinning blades on the
     NOUN   NUMBER

end of its metallic _____. "Leave this _____!" Blaze
    PART OF THE BODY   NOUN

yelled as she launched a barrage of fiery _____ at the robot,
          PLURAL NOUN

which _____ stumbled back. Dr. Eggman pressed a button,
   ADVERB

and his robot launched a swarm of mini _____ at Blaze.
         PLURAL NOUN

They spun through the air and fired _____ missiles at her. Blaze
      ADJECTIVE

_____ leaped up and spun through the air, smashing each one
ADVERB

with her mighty _____!
    NOUN

MAD LIBS® is fun to play with friends, but you can also play it by yourself! To begin with, DO NOT look at the story on the page below. Fill in the blanks on this page with the words called for. Then, using the words you have selected, fill in the blank spaces in the story.

Now you've created your own hilarious MAD LIBS® game!

STEP IT UP, PART 3

NOUN _____

VERB _____

NOUN _____

ADJECTIVE _____

NOUN _____

ADJECTIVE _____

PLURAL NOUN _____

PLURAL NOUN _____

PART OF THE BODY (PLURAL) _____

VERB (PAST TENSE) _____

NOUN _____

PLURAL NOUN _____

ADJECTIVE _____

VERB (PAST TENSE) _____

PLURAL NOUN _____

VERB _____

ADJECTIVE _____

NOUN _____

Sonic raced toward _____-side Island. He was running out of
<u>NOUN</u>

time to make Dr. Eggman _____ once and for all. Above him, he
<u>VERB</u>

could hear the sound of Tails' flying _____ closing in. Sonic
<u>NOUN</u>

felt _____ to have his best _____ by his side as he
<u>ADJECTIVE</u>   <u>NOUN</u>

faced off against Dr. Eggman's army of _____ robots. Standing
<u>ADJECTIVE</u>

in the distance, Sonic could see the giant metallic _____
<u>PLURAL NOUN</u>

blocking his path. They had large bodies that looked like angry

_____ with spiked _____ that smashed
<u>PLURAL NOUN</u>   <u>PART OF THE BODY (PLURAL)</u>

into the ground as they _____ forward. The Tornado,
<u>VERB (PAST TENSE)</u>

Tails' bi-winged _____, launched a volley of _____ at
<u>NOUN</u>   <u>PLURAL NOUN</u>

the robots. The explosions confused the _____ robots, and
<u>ADJECTIVE</u>

they _____ out of control, knocking their massive
<u>VERB (PAST TENSE)</u>

_____ into one another. Sonic used the distraction to quickly
<u>PLURAL NOUN</u>

_____ toward his target. He could see the _____
<u>VERB</u>   <u>ADJECTIVE</u>

Dr. Eggman in his command _____ in the distance.
<u>NOUN</u>

MAD LIBS® is fun to play with friends, but you can also play it by yourself! To begin with, DO NOT look at the story on the page below. Fill in the blanks on this page with the words called for. Then, using the words you have selected, fill in the blank spaces in the story.

Now you've created your own hilarious MAD LIBS® game!

I AM THE REAL SONIC

CELEBRITY _____

VERB _____

NOUN _____

NOUN _____

OCCUPATION _____

COLOR _____

NOUN _____

ADJECTIVE _____

NOUN _____

PART OF THE BODY _____

VERB ENDING IN "ING" _____

NOUN _____

PLURAL NOUN _____

ADJECTIVE _____

PERSON IN ROOM _____

A PLACE _____

ADJECTIVE _____

ADVERB _____

MAD LIBS

I AM THE REAL SONIC

Metal _____ may look like the real Sonic, and he might
          CELEBRITY

_____ just as fast as him, but this evil _____ is
    VERB   NOUN

nothing like our hero. This robotic _____ was created by
                                         NOUN

Dr. Eggman (who's not even a real _____!) to defeat our
                                    OCCUPATION

_____ hero and conquer places such as Pirate _____.
    COLOR   NOUN

This _____ version of Sonic is made completely out of
        ADJECTIVE

_____, and his robotic _____ can only think about
    NOUN   PART OF THE BODY

_____ Sonic. Metal Sonic once used the _____
  VERB ENDING IN "ING"   NOUN

Stones to travel through _____. Because of the Stones'
                            PLURAL NOUN

_____ power, Metal Sonic traveled back to a time before
    ADJECTIVE

_____ the Hedgehog existed. But Sonic stopped him before
  PERSON IN ROOM

he could change history and take over (the) _____ forever.
                                                A PLACE

Since then, each time Sonic encounters the _____ robot, he
                                              ADJECTIVE

_____ defeats him!
    ADVERB

MAD LIBS® is fun to play with friends, but you can also play it by yourself! To begin with, DO NOT look at the story on the page below. Fill in the blanks on this page with the words called for. Then, using the words you have selected, fill in the blank spaces in the story.

Now you've created your own hilarious MAD LIBS® game!

ALL THE WORLD'S GEMS ARE MINE

PART OF THE BODY (PLURAL) _____

PERSON IN ROOM _____

NOUN _____

ADJECTIVE _____

NOUN _____

ADJECTIVE _____

CELEBRITY _____

NOUN _____

PART OF THE BODY _____

NOUN _____

VERB (PAST TENSE) _____

NOUN _____

ADJECTIVE _____

VERB _____

PART OF THE BODY _____

EXCLAMATION _____

MAD LIBS®
ALL THE WORLD'S GEMS ARE MINE

Rouge the Bat flapped her powerful _____ and
<u>PART OF THE BODY (PLURAL)</u>

soared high above Team _____. Sonic and his friends were
<u>PERSON IN ROOM</u>

guarding a shiny _____ that would be a nice addition to her
<u>NOUN</u>

_____ collection of treasure. "You're not going to get past my
<u>ADJECTIVE</u>

_____!" yelled Sonic. But the _____ bat had a plan.
<u>NOUN</u>   <u>ADJECTIVE</u>

She spun around and flew directly at _____, who was closest
<u>CELEBRITY</u>

to the treasure. "That _____ is mine!" Rouge called out as she
<u>NOUN</u>

reached out her _____ and tried to grab the jewel. Amy Rose
<u>PART OF THE BODY</u>

grabbed the _____ and passed it to Tails, who _____
<u>NOUN</u>   <u>VERB (PAST TENSE)</u>

on a giant _____. Rouge knocked the _____ fox backward
<u>NOUN</u>   <u>ADJECTIVE</u>

and intercepted the treasure. But before she could _____ away, a
<u>VERB</u>

furry _____ reached out and snatched it away from her.
<u>PART OF THE BODY</u>

"Oh, _____!" Rouge cried out as she watched Sonic speed
<u>EXCLAMATION</u>

away!

MAD LIBS® is fun to play with friends, but you can also play it by yourself! To begin with, DO NOT look at the story on the page below. Fill in the blanks on this page with the words called for. Then, using the words you have selected, fill in the blank spaces in the story.

Now you've created your own hilarious MAD LIBS® game!

I WILL PROTECT THE FUTURE

ADJECTIVE _____

A PLACE _____

NOUN _____

ADJECTIVE _____

PLURAL NOUN _____

ADJECTIVE _____

VERB (PAST TENSE) _____

NUMBER _____

NOUN _____

PLURAL NOUN _____

ADJECTIVE _____

PERSON IN ROOM _____

PLURAL NOUN _____

PLURAL NOUN _____

PERSON IN ROOM _____

VERB _____

MAD☺LIBS®

I WILL PROTECT THE FUTURE

Something _____ has happened to (the) _____.
                ADJECTIVE   A PLACE

What was once a beautiful _____ has become _____
                              NOUN   ADJECTIVE

and unlivable. The _____ of the future decided that they
                      PLURAL NOUN

needed to prevent the _____ thing that happened to their
                           ADJECTIVE

world. So Silver _____ back in time _____ years
                    VERB (PAST TENSE)   NUMBER

to prevent the destruction. Now in the present, Silver uses his

_____ of psychokinesis—or the ability to manipulate
     NOUN

_____ using only his _____ brain—to fight
      PLURAL NOUN   ADJECTIVE

Dr. _____, who was responsible for ruining his world.
     PERSON IN ROOM

However, to defeat Dr. Eggman, he'll need the help of Sonic and his

team of _____. Although the two hedgehogs often argue
           PLURAL NOUN

over _____, Silver knows that he and _____ must
        PLURAL NOUN   PERSON IN ROOM

learn to _____ together in order to save his home!
            VERB

MAD LIBS® is fun to play with friends, but you can also play it by yourself! To begin with, DO NOT look at the story on the page below. Fill in the blanks on this page with the words called for. Then, using the words you have selected, fill in the blank spaces in the story.

Now you've created your own hilarious MAD LIBS® game!

TOTALLY AWESOME!

NOUN _____

NOUN _____

ADVERB _____

NOUN _____

ADJECTIVE _____

NOUN _____

PART OF THE BODY _____

ADJECTIVE _____

PART OF THE BODY _____

PERSON IN ROOM (MALE) _____

ADJECTIVE _____

PLURAL NOUN _____

CELEBRITY _____

ADJECTIVE _____

NOUN _____

PERSON IN ROOM _____

NOUN _____

MAD LIBS

TOTALLY AWESOME!

Have you misplaced your favorite _____? Has your Chao gone
_____NOUN

missing? Well, you've come to the right _____. Here at the
_____NOUN

Chaotix Detective Agency, we'll _____ solve any mystery
_____ADVERB

that's plaguing your _____. Our _____ leader,
_____NOUN_____ADJECTIVE

Vector, is one tough _____ with a super _____. But
_____NOUN_____PART OF THE BODY

don't let his _____ exterior fool you—underneath it all, he has
_____ADJECTIVE

a kind _____. And if you need something tracked down,
_____PART OF THE BODY

look no further than _____ Bee. Although he is
_____PERSON IN ROOM (MALE)

_____ and full of energy, Charmy Bee will stop at nothing to
ADJECTIVE

find your missing _____. The final member of the team is
_____PLURAL NOUN

_____ the Chameleon. This _____ ninja _____
CELEBRITY_____ADJECTIVE_____NOUN

is the agency's top investigator. He has the power to camouflage himself

and can spy on _____ by blending into the _____
_____PERSON IN ROOM_____NOUN

and hiding out of sight.

MAD LIBS® is fun to play with friends, but you can also play it by yourself! To begin with, DO NOT look at the story on the page below. Fill in the blanks on this page with the words called for. Then, using the words you have selected, fill in the blank spaces in the story.

Now you've created your own hilarious MAD LIBS® game!

BABYLON ROGUES

NOUN _____

ADVERB _____

A PLACE _____

ADJECTIVE _____

NOUN _____

NOUN _____

VERB ENDING IN "ING" _____

NOUN _____

NOUN _____

PERSON IN ROOM _____

ADJECTIVE _____

PLURAL NOUN _____

EXCLAMATION _____

PLURAL NOUN _____

ADJECTIVE _____

MAD LIBS®

BABYLON ROGUES

"Check out my Extreme _____ skills," Jet called out _____
                    NOUN   ADVERB

as he prepared for the upcoming _____ Grand Prix. "With
                                         A PLACE

this _____ Gear, I'll beat Sonic for sure. I'm the fastest
       ADJECTIVE

_____ out there. I plan to win the Grand Prix, and steal an
  NOUN

emerald _____, too!" "I don't know, Jet. We need to focus on
       NOUN

_____ and not on that speedy _____," said
VERB ENDING IN "ING"   NOUN

Wave. "But I have my _____ all ready to go," said Jet. "I've been
               NOUN

waiting for the Grand Prix, and I really want to show _____
                                  PERSON IN ROOM

who is _____. Can't we just race first and steal _____
     ADJECTIVE   PLURAL NOUN

later?" "_____!" cried Storm. "How about we let Boss beat
     EXCLAMATION

Sonic at the Grand Prix, while we steal the _____? Let's
                                  PLURAL NOUN

listen to Boss. He is the most _____ guy we know!"
                          ADJECTIVE

MAD LIBS® is fun to play with friends, but you can also play it by yourself! To begin with, DO NOT look at the story on the page below. Fill in the blanks on this page with the words called for. Then, using the words you have selected, fill in the blank spaces in the story.

Now you've created your own hilarious MAD LIBS® game!

STEP IT UP, PART 4

NOUN _____

COLOR _____

NOUN _____

PART OF THE BODY _____

ADJECTIVE _____

NOUN _____

NUMBER _____

PLURAL NOUN _____

VERB (PAST TENSE) _____

PLURAL NOUN _____

ADJECTIVE _____

NOUN _____

ADJECTIVE _____

EXCLAMATION _____

PART OF THE BODY _____

ADVERB _____

NOUN _____

ADJECTIVE _____

MAD LIBS

STEP IT UP, PART 4

Sonic raced toward the final _____ while Tails flew his
NOUN

_____ plane right above him. Standing in their way was yet
COLOR

another robotic _____, but this one had Dr. Eggman in a
NOUN

cockpit in the robot's _____. The villain laughed as he saw
PART OF THE BODY

Sonic and Tails heading his way. The _____ robot reared back
ADJECTIVE

and transformed into a metal _____ with _____ tentacles
NOUN   NUMBER

shooting out in all directions. Tails' plane crashed into the web of

_____. He leaped out and _____ toward the
PLURAL NOUN   VERB (PAST TENSE)

cockpit. Sonic dodged the robotic _____ that whipped
PLURAL NOUN

around him as he raced back and forth, causing the _____
ADJECTIVE

tentacles to tangle as the robotic _____ began to stumble. Dr.
NOUN

Eggman was _____ and cried out, "_____!" Sonic
ADJECTIVE   EXCLAMATION

climbed up the robot's mighty _____ and met Tails at the
PART OF THE BODY

cockpit. The two heroes smiled as Dr. Eggman _____ pounded
ADVERB

buttons, and the mighty robotic _____ fell forward. Once
NOUN

again, Dr. Eggman was _____!
ADJECTIVE